THE   VERTICAL

INTERROGATION

OF   STRANGERS

THE VERTICAL

INTERROGATION

OF STRANGERS

Bhanu Kapil

KELSEY ST. PRESS

FOR KIM FORTIER

Grateful acknowledgment is made to the editors of *In Short* where earlier versions of 72 and 81 first appeared.

Special thanks to Anthony Piccione, Laura Mullen, John Calderazzo and Carole Maso for their close readings; and to John Lucas, for making me write *Bad Mango*, a first attempt.

Library of Congress Cataloging-in-Publication Data

Kapil, Bhanu
    The vertical interrogation of strangers / Bhanu Kapil.
        p.   cm.
    ISBN 9780932716569 (pbk. :alk. paper)
      1. East Indian American women—Poetry. 2. Women, East Indian—England—Poetry. 3. Women—India—Poetry.   4. England—Poetry.   5. India—Poetry I. Title.
    PS3618.I39 V47 2001
    811.'6—dc21   2001029967

Cover image: untitled, 1998, by Acharya Vyakul, mixed media on paper.
Private collection, courtesy Lawrence Markey Gallery, New York.

Poulson/Gluck Design
The text is set in Minion.
Printed by McNaughton & Gunn

Kelsey St. Press   2824 Kelsey Street, Berkeley, California 94705
                       email: info@kelseyst.com   website: www.kelseyst.com

Distributed by: Small Press Distribution   800-869-7553   email: orders@spdbooks.org

**NATIONAL
ENDOWMENT
FOR THE ARTS**   Publication of this book was made possible in part
by grants from the National Endowment for the Arts
and the California Arts Council.

Because she arrives, vibrant, over and over again; we are at the beginning of a new history, or rather a process of becoming in which several histories intersect with one another. As a subject for history, woman always occurs simultaneously in several places. (In woman, personal history blends together with the history of all women, as well as national and world history.)

I wished that woman would write and proclaim this unique empire so that other women, other unacknowledged sovereigns, might exclaim: I too, overflow; my desires have invented new desires, my body knows unheard of songs. Time and again, I too, have felt so full of luminous torrents I could burst — burst with forms much more beautiful than those which are put up in frames and sold for a stinking fortune.

— Hélène Cixous, Utopias

INTRODUCTION

From January 12, 1992, to June 4, 1996, I traveled in India, England, and the United States, interviewing Indian women of diverse ages and backgrounds. Originally, my question to them was, "Is it possible for you to say the thing you have never been able to say, not even to the one you have spent your whole life loving?" Over the course of the last four years I asked these women — strangers I met in theaters, forests, laundromats, temples and diners — to respond more specifically to one or more of a predetermined selection of twelve questions. They agreed, on the condition of anonymity, to submit a spoken (tape-recorded) or written response in thirty minutes. During this half hour, the questionee was locked in a room without windows, furniture, or overhead lighting. My aim was to ensure an honest and swift text, uncensored by guilt or the desire to construct an impressive, publishable "finish." In editing this anthology of responses, I did not attempt to "clean up" their roughness or rawness in terms of syntax, grammar, spelling, punctuation, or the way in which they filled the space of the page. The only alterations I made were in converting responses, or parts of responses, into English.

— The project as I thought it would be:
an anthology of the voices of Indian women.

As I traveled between the countries of my birth (England), ancestry (India), and residence (America), I answered the questions for myself again and again. My responses were set down in a notebook, on scraps, or written on stickers that I affixed to escalator tubing, café tables, shop windows. The voices of the women I met: pure sound. The shapes they made, as they moved through the world: methods. A way to describe my body. I didn't know where I was going.

— The project as I wrote it: a tilted plane.

TWELVE QUESTIONS

1. Who are you and whom do you love?

2. Where did you come from / how did you arrive?

3. How will you begin?

4. How will you live now?

5. What is the shape of your body?

6. Who was responsible for the suffering of your mother?

7. What do you remember about the earth?

8. What are the consequences of silence?

9. Tell me what you know about dismemberment.

10. Describe a morning you woke without fear.

11. How will you / have you prepare(d) for your death?

12. And what would you say if you could?

1. WHAT IS THE SHAPE OF YOUR BODY?

Sometimes in the spaces, there is fear. Choose one:
1. The body of a woman, how she moves through the day.
2. Inside her: lolling oblongs, a little runny.
3. As seen through the mosquito net.
4. The translucencies of Sigmar Polke.
5. I don't know anything.

Artificial resin, lacquer on synthetic fabric. Substances that caused the surface to change colour. Silver oxide, red lead, cobalt chloride. Lanterns. Transparent polyester. Layered washes of lacquered colours and resins.

I don't know where to begin. But I know

my elbow, my back tooth: throbbing

I must.

1. *How she moves*
"I keep looking over my left shoulder, to see if he's still there."

My name, my body. Such versions, I occupy. Live in, as surely as a dung-wall house, a house that does not turn, is not born twice: skulls, oranges. A ladder leaning against a eucalyptus tree. A black hen with her red beak, in a basket of straw in the tree next to the front door of the house. Where I live. With a man whose one eyebrow joins together. (Blown ash.) Plum blossoms. Mango orchard. Rooster. Two eggs; bees. A very dark brown horse. A clay oven. Honey. The sun. A cinnamon liqueur, he brings me. I gulp then sleep, stunned by the sweetness of nouns. He has made altars of peacock feathers, *paise*, tiny mirrors, a dried stem of jasmine that is taller than I am. Then I'm awake. Wild salt of his chest and belly. A bed.

It may be that I have taken an irreversible action. (Woody smoke.) A goat skin drying on the clothes line.

2. Her body
I risk lemons. I risk melted honey. I risk water. I risk an old wine bottle that has the shape of a Dravidian goddess. Her abandoned torso. Her hips. The massive sloping stubs of her transparent shoulders: I risk. The green glass of this body walking, slowly, along the orchard path. Balancing the lemonade on my head.

3. Her eyes
It is difficult today. The orchard. (Making something.) I see making a shape there. Dragging a black tarp under the farthest mango tree, over the old skins and nettles. I began to. But stopped.

4. Her surface

Red clay. A dry river-bed. I'm scared of the dogs. I'm scared of the cow-men. No. I'm not from here. My hair loosely braided, oily, not kempt. My body gets smokey. Gets holes in it; its layers of bright cotton. No. I was, without a doubt, born in an English-speaking country. A country I could no longer tolerate.

5. What she knows

Shame may be fatal. I am here now. How I got here: gravity. The long dark of the border of Pakistan and India. Speed faster than colour. Not being a man, I bleed like this. To arrive seasonal, in pain, not what he thought.

I am not beautiful. I couldn't even look into the faces of the air hostesses. Only the darkness around them. At a slant.

I write because I cannot paint.

Salt. Rose. The colour black between the stars, beneath tongues. The darkness of our bedroom when we blow out the candles. The coals and the ash in the *ingiti* at dusk. The sound of a man working with nails and a hammer, as I write this. Later, after *chai*, we'll have our bath. Salt crystals from Goa. Rose-water from an Indian grocery shop in the East End of London. It is difficult. He is always with me. These are the scraps.

2. WHO ARE YOU AND WHOM DO YOU LOVE?

A month from now. A week from now. Tomorrow. When he goes. The going. I'll make crepes, walk by the river with the dog, float candles in a pudding basin; the usual. He's gone. Between our bodies: the sun at 5 a.m.; fifty-seven Herefords, and a Brahma bull that broke the river fence; four and a half thousand hummingbirds; a dying man; a man who is about to knock on the door of a woman with black eyes, to tell her that he loves her; the woman herself, who is drawing a bath. She can't hear the door above the water. And her eyes aren't really black. They're brown. She lights a match.

Floating candles. The incommensurable distance. I forgot to memorize his face.

3. DESCRIBE A MORNING YOU WOKE WITHOUT FEAR.

The Ganges at Hardwar. Dusk. Steps. For two rupees, I buy a boat of palm leaves. It holds a diva: tiny earthenware pot, oil, a wick. I light a match. Push the boat into the river with my hands. Years later, the Pacific foam boiling at my feet, invisible whales migrating north, like the stars at daybreak, I try to remember that night. That version of water. I can't.

I remember the oiliness of my fingertips, and the smell of human flesh, upriver, burning. Frothy crusts, steam: the smell, also, of hot milk being poured, brass bowl to brass bowl, *dudh*, thick syllable, at the top of the steps. How I sat for hours, drinking the hot, sweet, milky tea, my last night there before I headed south, to Jaipur. A red desert. The opposite of a sea. Its aftermath.

4. WHERE DID YOU COME FROM /
HOW DID YOU ARRIVE?

"May I?"

"If you'd like."

"What are you writing about?"

"Nothing."

"I've been watching you."

"What do I look like, then?"

"I don't know. Your hair keeps falling over your face. Are you
  Muslim or something?"

"No. Zoroaster."

"Zarathustra?"

"I'm not a member of a cult."

And then, the names I'd never heard before: Brecht, Eno, Klimt. A
night and a day and a night on this train: talking, smoking: Afghani
biris by the window, blowing the green smoke through the bars, into
a landscape of red dust and tangled stumps. The occasional blur of
a peacock diving off the tracks; blue-green, like taffeta: and then his
face: coarse, pocky skin, the roughness of his nose and lips. (The
trees were dead.) But full. What he was saying: Afrikaaner-Dutch,
Dutch-English: the constant, voluptuous *ya*.

Years later, walking, in the freezing London cold, I went into a Turkish
school for immigrants, to warm my hands. I sat on the windowsill
in a room high above the canal: looking down, I saw a woman bicy-
cle past, a cello strapped to her back in its black case. It resembled
the carapace of an insect about to rupture its shiny skin. I should
have seen my future then, in the way that woman carried what she
loved along the length of her spine: her home / kept moving.

5. HOW WILL YOU LIVE NOW?

Like this. Brightly. Growing brighter. As the pink ore of Shivalik glows, at dusk. It lasts for five minutes. I have hands: counting always by the three horizontal creases inside each finger. Marking with the thumb. Fourteen. Seconds. He taught me this. How to tell time by my body. Sometimes I want to tell him: I do not understand what you are saying. Instead, I disguise my slowness: asking him, brightly, if he would like another cup of *chai*.

6. HOW WILL YOU LIVE NOW?

I wake in the peristaltic predawn — purple-black, navy-blue, blue — to say good-bye. He drinks some water. Puts his glass down on my bookshelf. Turns.

It takes three days for the remaining water to evaporate. Because it is winter, I don't open the window, and so, for weeks, I breathe in a constantly circulating invisibility. I convince myself such things are true by counting my in-breaths and then counting my out-breaths, per minute, then minutes, then hour. *Om eying hareeng kleeng char moonday ye biche: om eying hareeng kleeng* — This goes on until I dream myself as ribs. Four ribs, floating in a body of air. Bird calls. Nausea. The terrifying absence of a stomach, or a throat, or a plastic bucket.

7. WHAT ARE THE CONSEQUENCES OF SILENCE?

Again, nothing. The sky above New York is thick red. I wrote to you but you did not reply. How difficult and corny, checking mail each night. *Nicht*. The paper I wrote on was yellow and clotted with fibres. My nib caught, sometimes, mid-sentence; I wrote:

No, I can't say it. You live somewhere beyond the marrow of / the scarlet, cortical — *this*. You live somewhere, and there's a dried cream-scum — sea-shore — around the rim of your cup. *Which* sea? I don't know whether I should face east, or west.

8. WHAT DO YOU REMEMBER ABOUT THE EARTH?

In the absence of Cézannes, I stare at the wavering light world: Venus rising over the hogbacks; the copper striations along the banks of the Colorado river; a waitress's worn stockings; their heels, the light of her body; shop awnings, as seen through Viennese blinds, from a window table. I am trying to keep my heart open. No need to slit the soles of my feet. This is the earth. This is my one jumping life. We began the day in snow. Now the sage. (*How I've missed you.*) A few quick notes, then: To live without fear. South. I open and open. He writes: *you greedy cow.*

9. WHAT ARE THE CONSEQUENCES OF SILENCE?

Harbour. Fresh brown eggs. Curlicue anemones. The songs of whales.

It is difficult to write about love.

Lapsang souchong tea. Smoked chilies. The maps of Utah and New Mexico. Alfalfa bales. And then the cows. A hundred or more: Hereford, Limousine, Brahma. I stare into two hundred eyes at once. We are traveling east, and inland, for the last, or first, time in our lives. I am twenty-five years old.

He writes: *I am thirty-two years old.*

The tea tastes of bark, and wood-smoke.

You have not written one word about what happened between us. (In a South African accent.)

The cows cross the river to give birth at the end of each winter. They break the fence, and they swim. I will never eat beef again.

10. HOW WILL YOU / HAVE YOU PREPARE(D) FOR YOUR DEATH?

Moab. A white South African man and a brown-skinned English-woman walk up a ridge towards the Delicate Arch. No. They aren't walking towards anything. When they see the surreal orange loop, they are both shocked. Having come to this place without guide-books. Map: there is a sudden precipice, then a coiled valley of red-dish stone. He walks on ahead. Later he tells her he rubbed and tugged at his penis as hard as he could: spurting: arc after arc: of semen, over the edge. Later, in front of the motel mirror, as she is pulling on her trousers: *let your fear adore you. It wants to get you off.* She still doesn't know what he means. She is drinking milky tea in the Café Vertigo in Green Park, and she is thinking that her body is not in one straight line. He is still fast asleep on a mattress next to the kerosene heater, and it is winter, and she will never tell him these things. She will never tell him about her body; she will simply kneel, continue to kneel, next to the low bed, a bowl of foamy coffee between her cupped hands, as if she is asking for something, and she is: waiting for him to wake up. Waking, he reaches for her. Her knees are raw. She closes her eyes. It is her habit. He flicks his tongue over her lips. The yoghurt-smell of his sleep-breath. She kisses him with a kiss she learned from books. Sticky. Sometimes, for days, weeks even, she forgets that she is going to die.

11.   WHERE DID YOU COME FROM /
HOW DID YOU ARRIVE?

Notes on being a nomad:

1. We drank the colour blue from iridescent glasses. This would never happen again, as long as I lived.

2. I felt huge, as if, when I lived there, I must have been a very little girl. Opening my old wardrobe, I saw the buckled shelf I used to lie on, smothered by my clothes, when my mother started up again.

3. He said: you are my home.

4. Customs: I feel very far away, even though they are just beyond the glass barriers. My mother. My father. I can't see them. It can't be glass. Plastic? No, not plastic. Something else. They're gone. No. *I'm* gone.

5. There are no faces like yours in this country.

6. A wine stain on the paper. A letter from my father: "The idea is to go from day to day, from week to week, from month to month, for the first eight months."

7. I dream of babies, they fly out of my arms. What's that? "We die, my darling, we die." Yes, but do you love me? "You're avoiding the subject." Yes, but what kind of child was I? I can't remember anything.

8. No, I couldn't. I couldn't hold, not able to, impossible really, under the circs.

9. They fly out of my arms. I fly out of their arms.

12.   HOW WILL YOU BEGIN?

Flying from Heathrow to JFK, I see below, an unknown arctic landscape of black mountains and white rivers. The sky is pale blue, darkening to an indigo that contains black, but isn't black, at the edge of sight. At the same time, the sun is shining brightly. (The world is everything at once.)

13. TELL ME WHAT YOU KNOW ABOUT DISMEMBERMENT.

The pelvic bone, found in the back field, in Taos. When you were a woman with black thighs, who walked for hours through the sage, because, *quiero vivir,* you wanted to live.

The February morning you turned your face away from what you secretly loved, and why? (Waking at first light after two hours of sleep, the real rose turning into an actual light; we sink back into the oil-stained sheets. *And how?*)

You want to live? Finally, you're alone. The ice drifts in the hollows. You walked here. The sheer maroon cliffs. The silver bones of your pelvis. The bright blue sky. Your bloodstone. This water. Something huge and without music has just happened.

How do you know the bones of your pelvis are the colour of the moon? The human moon? The moon above New Mexico?

Because he can taste my menstrual blood. Because we kiss.

To cube life. Because we can't take it — in a whole form. We are not cobras. (Voluptuous swallowers.) *Are we?* He lays out the strips of goat meat on the wooden slab.

14. DESCRIBE A MORNING YOU WOKE WITHOUT FEAR.

Honey on my right eye. Monarch wing stuck to the lid. 5:20 a.m. I sit up, facing the glass-pines, the dark slope of snow. This is the woods, then, and he has pressed closer; nuzzles his face against my knee. Rubs his forehead against the bone. I must live by these sentences. Writing is dangerous.

I have built a fire and poured hot water over my mugwort leaves in a mason jar. *Then live in love. Then wake up.* I am bleeding heavily. I'm learning how to leave the love-bed, the sound of pine-wind rushing up the slope, the sweetness of his sleep-face, against my knee: and come upstairs, and make a fire, and write.

15. AND WHAT WOULD YOU SAY IF YOU COULD?

Or: a little tongue slips out. The eyes are aslant. There are horns. A candle embedded in the skull. *Who have you spent your whole life loving?*

Or: her hair falls in a curved lineage of colour and air. Black / Wyoming. More of a tree-black than the one I'd always imagined: unstriated, up there, a little spotty. Wyoming: impossible lunar wind. A woman, getting up from a chair. Slope on slope. The process of standing. She took days to paint.

And now the cantata begins, in the hull of an American cathedral. When I open my eyes, one of the luscious, vampirical basses holds my looking. I don't look away. My womb, my nails, the blood of it. There's no going back to how it was. The music does this to us, and when it ends, I make, I move to make, an epileptic's reentry into time. The others. The stranger. His song. Then a gobbling silence. The street. The word, *street.*

16. HOW WILL YOU / HAVE YOU
PREPARE(D) FOR YOUR DEATH?

Sometimes a man says something to a woman, and after that she knows she is incapable of giving birth to something. That would live.

For days, I wrote about a woman whose lungs were filled with water. I made, instead, the body of the man standing at the edge of the river. Matted lashes. Flush irises. He has my eyes. The last time I saw him, I kissed his chest, through his shirt. Silk. Violet. And that was before I knew what my life would be like, without him. It was before the phone rang, and I did not reply, not even a year later, on the corner, when someone asked me if I wanted milk or sugar.

Beneath ideas: the tightness in the chest at the beginning of a long sentence, the fuschia spikes of closed eyelids, dismembered kisses, arbitrary thirsts. Milk. Something sweet. *Please.*

17.   HOW WILL YOU BEGIN?

The sides of my mouth taste of licorice. 2 p.m. I'm still wearing my pajamas. There's so much, and I can't begin. Sometimes, I want to stick my pen in the arms of people who bore me. Every morning, I wake up, put water on for my tea, flip my Edith Piaf tape, clear a space at the table. I don't want to write stories anymore. I am not a stripper.

"Well, you go in, and if you get in before six o'clock, it's free. After that, it's ten bucks. There's three stages. Front stage, back stage, and The Jungle Gym. My arms are pretty strong so I do okay in The Jungle Gym. I don't do lap dances, but I'm thinking, I can save $12,000 by June, then take off. Maybe Santa Cruz. Maybe Chico."

18. HOW WILL YOU / HAVE YOU PREPARE(D) FOR YOUR DEATH?

Sometimes you feel very pleased to be on the move again. Sometimes you miss your father so badly, you dream of an opaque ocean filled with pink flamingos. Your father is waiting for you in a café with striped awnings on the far shore. He is eating fish and chips, and pomegranates. You swim and swim. When you reach the sand, he's gone. You take his battered brown shoes in your arms one by one, cradling them like the littlest ones with the flapping dusty tongues, the ones you have to bring inside, to wean.

19. AND WHAT WOULD YOU SAY IF YOU COULD?

I loved him according to the law of fishes. The sole devours the sprat. Another thing about fishes: they are constantly submerged in the element of their waking. But then what? The katabasis of the earth-bound, who will never shine: muddy rubies, the eyes of the dead.

I keep forgetting to breathe. The eyes of the living, then, on the trains that stop at all points of a circle. The Circle Line. The Northern Line. Victoria. (The sequined bodice of a woman in the swinging aisle. As we enter the tunnel, the lights dim. She is invisible, except for the aqueous after-image of her torso, which recedes, then flares, then fades, then reappears, abruptly, when the lights pop on.)

Underground, ANGEL, I think of Rilke, that bright face, inches from the ore. EMBANKMENT: the stone stairwells of St. Paul's cathedral, gleaming and darkening and turning, on a Tuesday afternoon. PIMLICO: the doors hiss and clack. The street shines with a fledgling snow. Steps. A door. I go in, take off my coat. There he is. The huge, translucent, amber-streaked cock of Esptein's angel, hanging down between his thighs. How the angel heaves Jacob into his arms, his body of light. White cells streaming, deep in the glorious, stalled marble.

20. TELL ME WHAT YOU KNOW ABOUT DISMEMBERMENT.

The disaster is the gift. And it was. The old coat sniffed over and over, but. Standing up in the closet. As if someone had died. (An affidavit of smell.) I don't know how to avoid this sweetness.

His coat was made of rain, and the torn-off covers of English paperbacks, and human hair. It smelled of the earth, then; the twin histories of nostalgia, and bone-snapping. Who are the bone-snappers? How did one end up, backed into this corner, staring hard at the scuffed toes of one's boots, avoiding the eyes of the sodden, brilliantined power rangers? (I was cold. He put his coat around my shoulders. He walked me home. I made us a nice bit of tomato soup, out of a can. It was raining. He asked me if I liked the novels of Anita Brookner. I said no. He said my hair smelled of snow. I said yes.)

21.   DESCRIBE A MORNING YOU WOKE WITHOUT FEAR.

One pretends not to be free. Saying: I can't. When he came to America, he was appalled by the inelegance of this country's public buildings, saying: it is not my culture. Then he returned to the little glazed cakes and exquisite leaded glass portholes of Europe.

As if our responsibilities to each other end at the border of our countries, or at our cities, or half-way across our cities, or at our back doors, or at our skins. *No.*

22. DESCRIBE A MORNING YOU WOKE WITHOUT FEAR.

I don't know how to measure this. Item: he's drinking espresso romano from a paper cup. Item: he's sucking on, then spitting out, the bright peel. Item: it's late. His teeth are a little smashed. He's practicing for something, as always. Now what? I can see the paper moving between his fingers, his lips moving. (But I remember when I took him to me: a railway station, a red desert. Two, three, four, five a.m. I barely know him. A wooden bench. Someone is boiling milk behind us, on a tiny stove. A coal bucket. The smell of crushed cinnamon bark. Green cardamom pods. He rests his head in my lap. My hand, like a bird, hesitates. Then I stroke his thick blonde hair, until he falls asleep.) Sometimes you have to choose who you are.

23. HOW WILL YOU / HAVE YOU
     PREPARE(D) FOR YOUR DEATH?

Aurangabad: train-smoke in our eyes. A taxi. The young woman with black, oily hair wound and pinned writes our names in pencil. A disintegrating ledger and above her: unframed watercolours. Scenes from the fairy-tales of Oscar Wilde: *"And then — a giant — next to the wall — crying"*; and a small pen, in the garden her room opens into, for gazelles. Sliding our passports across the desk. (The lovely ones leaping, over and over, inside the one possible shape of their leaping.)

The only woman. A women's dormitory. A bed draped with nets. Heat and wetness. Lifting the white gauze, he said: *I could stop if you wanted to, but I won't try again. It's up to you.*

Roughness of the ropes against my back: yute bed, and the skin inside my body, rubbery: *ya:* the nets are dripping/his bones are: *ya,* he says, *ya:* collapses. And then the blood. On his palm, smoothing my hair. And then he gets it: the blood in my folds, the spaces between his fingers, the sheet. Stands up. Lights a candle. *Jesus. Why didn't you tell me?*

Waking alone. Rain in my shins, my ribs, the back of my head. He's wrapped the nets around me.

I put my hand between my thighs, and press.

24. HOW WILL YOU BEGIN?

When he was gone, I didn't speak for two months. *Shut up. Put your keys in your pocket. It's time to go.* The rain is soft. The rain is hard. I don't know anything. In the language we made up one night, the word for lover was the same as the word for a neatly folded manuscript you don't look at for a year. *There are many manuscripts. Some of them will tell you what your face will look like when you die, or when you marry someone who does not see your secret face. Some of them will give you certain instructions that, having read, you must follow, or else forget.* I'm walking, I'm walking then.

25. TELL ME WHAT YOU KNOW ABOUT DISMEMBERMENT.

I walked past the window of the antique shop two or three times a
week, on my way to the university. It was always shut. Its location,
on the corner of a brick terrace, in a northern English market town,
in a neighborhood of Gudjrati steel-workers, always seemed a little
irrational. The morning it was actually open, I went in;

(Dark. The northern rain, out. A woman of about sixty is sewing up
a hem. It's a wedding dress: imploded, a bit ragged. She lets me try
it on. It holds the half-light in its transparent, slightly torn layers.)

I always thought I'd marry in red, or pink, or orange: the colour of
the rising sun. A fire, silver-wrapped sweet-balls, my mumma, my
dad. Instead, because I did not want to return to England, I was
married in the white dress I'd bought across the sea: in the pouring
rain, under a crab-apple tree, next to a pond of Canadian geese, who
were resting for the summer, before heading south.

26. WHO ARE YOU AND WHOM DO YOU LOVE?

I wake up in his arms, but he doesn't let go, and he isn't smiling. It's a sort of wedding night. There isn't a ceremony. No henna. No black flowers on my eyelids. No freshly baked pastries filled with raspberry syrup. No stranger arriving on a horse. No wine. I dress in black-blue, climb over a wall into my neighbor's garden. Crouch down near the roots of a pine.

An hour later, an owl begins to sing to his owl-wife who lives on the other side of the city, but tonight she does not answer. So I sing. I think, that'll be nice, I'll sing, I can tell him I sang.

But my throat: shuts. I go back to the house, take my shoes off, get into bed. He flicks off the tape — the weirdo, unchained Bach — the mood music.

Someone has circled the word — almost — with a red pen. There's a question mark, and a little smile face, with no nose.

27. WHO IS RESPONSIBLE FOR
THE SUFFERING OF YOUR MOTHER?

August, 1967. My father returns to Punjab in the shiny black suit from Marks and Spencer.

My mother almost married the son of The Royal Baker of Rajhasthan, who baked, daily, pita breads and almond pastries, for the Maharani of Jaipur. But he was wearing white sneakers when he came to visit her. My mother told her father that she couldn't possibly marry someone who couldn't be bothered to polish his shoes.

Then my father arrives, and says: "I'm leaving for Europe in two weeks." My mother says: "But how can I marry a man who wears socks with red and blue stripes?" But her father, who is tired of placing ads in *The Indian Express* (M.A. Brahmin Girl, Lovely and Fair, Seeks Professional Brahmin Boy, A.S.A.P.), says: "But his feet are so white!"

It's true. My father's feet are hairy, but, nonetheless, after five English summers, ensconced in luridly patterned socks, wonderfully pale. When he takes naps, local urchins sneak into the courtyard, lift up the mosquito net, peer and giggle at these mysterious, creamcoloured appendages.

By the end of the summer, my mother is living in a one-room damp-walled walk-up in Hayes, Middlesex, where George Orwell once taught grammar school English, and where a thirteen-year-old skinhead called Stephen Whitby pours milk bottles of urine into the black — the Paki, the Bangladeshi, the Sri Lankan, the Ugandan, the Ethiopian, the Jamaican, and the Gudjrati — letter boxes.

28. WHERE DID YOU COME FROM / HOW DID YOU ARRIVE?

I don't know how this corresponds to the world: I miss his letters arriving, holding them between my fingertips like stems: the minutes before I open them, regardless of this morning, of never again being able to...

Sometimes you may never see your home again. An ache in the lower back, the methodical preparation of basil soup, the sweetness of the juice of the broken stems. I cover my face with my hands. Breathe in. When the violet colour comes, I leave my house, without shoes. This hour's so hungry. (The last things — the silk of his shirt, my forehead pressed to his chest, when I could not look at him, the glass or bone or threshold of his chest — are the ones I keep.)

I think of my mother, as a bride, leaving India. The softness of the tip of her nose, her brow, breasts, red palms pressed to the glass: she is staring at the tar steaming after rain. (The black water of her eyes falling in lines.)

29. WHO IS IT YOU HAVE SPENT YOUR WHOLE LIFE LOVING?

Clairvoyance: (Because he kisses you, your face turns coppery, the colour of the faces of Tibetans.) When the red colour comes, you are free of winter, its bony longings.

The body does not breathe in time: when you unfolded yourself, that first night, you broke the news of his kiss. (Red flower of the birth body / the tiny fist closing around the extended finger.) I don't remember anything else about the future.

(It is the future, a future where tongues are made of water. Tea. A fire. The anti-clockwise circling of the diamond-shaped mountain. He kisses me. *Let the sea:* he writes: *I can't help but let the sea: exit my body.*)

30. WHAT ARE THE CONSEQUENCES OF SILENCE? / WHAT DO YOU REMEMBER ABOUT THE EARTH?

A book, apparently there is a book — I want to make the book of looking for this book — the book of everything that has happened, of everything that will happen. Twenty-four shapes of longing. An abandoned alphabet. Each kiss, each sutured return to the origin.

My grandfather tried to return all his life, but couldn't. When I was nine years old, he took me with him, north, through the forests of Himachal, towards Gangotri. (The faces of bamboo-gatherers, appearing, then disappearing, behind the trees: red-orange streaks along the cheek-flats: Bhutanese, or Tibetan, nomads, border-slipping, they shared their milk with us; dri-milk, something I'd never tasted before; thus, sensual; acrid, like Russian egg-curd, but thin, watery. We drank it from shallow wooden bowls. Nobody said anything. Those forests were pale gold and green, curiously quiet and spacious, like rooms.)

We turned back after three weeks, skinny, our legs all scratched up. Glottal dialects, no birdsong, certain danger to the north. A book, we were looking for, of paper, we wanted, made, of flower-grasses.

31. WHERE DID YOU COME FROM /
HOW DID YOU ARRIVE?

The classic Agra honeymoon: A man built a tomb for his wife so he could see it from his prison window. My mother said: "I saw a woman's face; and her arms, and her shoulders. She must have floated down the Yamuna from the colony. Those untouchables can't even be bothered to burn their dead. Dirty old things. Your father? He wanted to go back to the hotel room. Hotel Peacock. All night long, he kept biting me. He bit me all over my tummy. I think, well yes, that's when, you were: *inside my body, once and for all.*"

Jammed between a Kuwaiti advertising executive and a Chinese girl from Vancouver: red wine in a plastic cup, and an on-going supply of damp, scented towellettes. A bifocal porthole, through which the Arabian Sea turns green, then red. One hour to Bombay. Somebody is asking me the question. I reply, "Coffee, please," and the moonlight turns into pure red sun, and then the clouds, and then the earth.

32. TELL ME WHAT YOU KNOW ABOUT DISMEMBERMENT.

History of an outstretched arm: In the morning, the Indian woman, a woman of about fifty-one years old, walked to the train station, bought a one-day underground pass. From Pimlico, south of the river, she walked to the Tate Gallery. Room 18. She stood for two hours in front of the painting of a woman in a low boat, candles blowing, a storm coming up, and a tower beginning to crumble behind her. "The Lady of Shallot." Oil. Waterhouse. The size of a wall.

The guard barely noticed her. He'd seen it before. Middle-aged hippies sitting cross-legged in front of the blurred, spooky Rothkos; young women with black lips coming back five days in a row, with their hard-backed spiral notebooks, to make geometric, smudgy drawings of Picasso's junkyard goat.

Which is why, when the woman raised her right arm, stretched it towards the painting, a paring knife in her right fist, the guard was staring down at the backs of his hands, examining the deplorable condition of his nails.

The golden light in the trees.

The stone-coloured fabric beneath them.

33. TELL ME WHAT YOU KNOW ABOUT DISMEMBERMENT.

Her blue dress, cut open, hung off her like torn petals after a hard summer rain. It was a hard summer. She had cut her dress off her own body with nail scissors. Now she was sitting at the edge of her bed, her back curved, her eyes itchy, her dress around her waist. She had been unable to unbutton it, and she had been hot. Now she was not as hot as she had been.

She was struck by lightning on the veranda, just as she was lifting the mint julep to her lips. Her mother found her like that: angled elbow, pursed lips, eyelids closed, upright, as if she were still alive. They had to cut her out of her blue dress.

She was wearing a blue dress. It was blue blue blue. I have wanted to write about her, but can't. Sometimes I think I should be writing about the chest itself: split open, and the violet colour pouring out. A Francis Bacon of a woman's torso. The inner skin, inverted, with its texture of over-ripe persimmons. The fruit falling off the bone. An oval bone you can hold in your fist like a thumb. The mount of Venus at the base of the thumb.

Last night, staring at the green planet, I wanted to say everything. That's not it either. A brush. This wrist. These shoulder blades. I write because I cannot paint.

34. WHAT IS THE SHAPE OF YOUR BODY?

Angel: an intense tension in her left shoulder blade, as if she is growing a wing. I know that she experiences her mouth as a smeared gesture: paint, fingers. In words, then?

Sometimes she feels that her body is open to the air. There is nothing that separates her from herself. She does not exist. She *can't* exist. If she existed, her wholeness would be irrelevant; a lit match. She's watching it burn. It burns like cream. As soon as she writes these things, she knows they are not true. *Angel.* The only word she knows in Spanish. *Smoky gelatin.* Everything is different now.

35. WHAT ARE THE CONSEQUENCES OF SILENCE?

The bed pushed, each night, against the door. Sometimes, in the evenings, the priest from the church on the corner walks my mother home. His mouth is like the tip of a penis: a lipless, inward opening. My mother has been singing ghazals in the crypt. She says it has the acoustics of a temple in Punjab. She doesn't use the word, acoustics. The priest want to know where my father is. *Interiors.* My father is drinking cheap whiskey in north Wales. He is studying linguistics. On weekends, he sits out on the back steps, smoking Silk Cuts, making some kind of incomprehensible decision about his life, about the kind of death that life will lead to. No feeling in my forehead, or my wrists, or my lower set of teeth, or the bone between my breasts.

Before: It is early morning, I am eating soggy corn flakes. My father, I see him out of the corner of my eye, I put my fingers in my ears, my mother has long black-grey hair that smells of coconut oil, and my father, no, my mother's saying something, and my father, I can tell even though I'm in the next room, I can see through the walls: he has a little foam, packed hard around his tongue.

36. DESCRIBE A MORNING YOU WOKE WITHOUT FEAR.

He's gone. This nest of sheets. Undouched, insomniac, winey, I keep the wine next to my bed. The occasional Republican swig. I don't know how else to honour ellipsis. The perpetual turquoise makes me nervous. When night comes, I take it easy. No fist of blood not gathering. No speaking of this broken thing to others. No bearing of it. I balk and balk, waking from naps with snake-mouth. Two a.m., though, and there's still some blue in the sky. And I still saw my father take my mother's hair in his right fist. That's nothing. The constant flinching. But I did not look away.

37. TELL ME WHAT YOU KNOW ABOUT DISMEMBERMENT.

So I look him in the eyes. There is nothing else to do. In the absence of direct electrical light, the interrogations become abstract. His questions grow eyes. I open and close my mouth very slowly. I can tell by the way he eats his Snickers that I'm beginning to get to him. He freezes each bar for at least five hours, before cutting it into slices with a paring knife. Each slice is very cold, so he has to eat it swiftly, between his back teeth, in a bossy, sparkly sort of way. Sparkle: anything that hasn't recently been dug up. The opposite of a corpse. Something you could buy on the home shopping channel.

He looks at me, and I can tell, by the twitching skin under his right eye, that it's going to start up again. The hoarding, the beakiness. Lately, my body feels more and more like a box.

38. WHAT IS THE SHAPE OF YOUR BODY?

The feeling of my body. I feel like the man who is making a pathway through a forest of thorns. He wants to reach a place that does not exist until he touches it with his mouth.

She has been sleeping for a long time. Brown crystals, like sugar, in the corners of her eyes. Her dreaming saliva has dried on her cheek, where it drizzled from her mouth. There are sparrows singing in the tree outside her window. People are shouting and embracing, as if they hadn't seen each other in years. Then they remember.

When they open the door, he. Has sunk his nails. Into her hip. She is pressing. Her hand against. Her eye. Smearing it. Her hand. Against the wall.

They tear the man out of her body.

I am thinking of the man, how he reminds me of Christ: the bloody one; the lover who is torn from his beloved; the stranger who brings the gift of awakening, but who is executed at dawn; the exhausted traveler.

39. HOW WILL YOU LIVE NOW?

They travel for days. Sometimes it rains abruptly. Silver flashes. The girl looks for eyes in the puddles after these sudden storms. She finds them: handfuls of monsoon frogs. Tiny. Bright-green, with bronze-brown flecks. She shows them to her grandfather. "Can we take them home?" *No.*

When she is grown, she realizes that she has forgotten everything. How to live without explanations. How to travel light. How to let the earth go. How skin can see.

40. WHAT IS THE SHAPE OF YOUR BODY? /
DESCRIBE A MORNING YOU WOKE WITHOUT FEAR.

The politics of the membrane: there are pathways from the outside
to the inside, and back again. The delirious spaces between atoms.
Unmentionable: the ephemerality of noses, gills, belly-buttons, and
the blue-green vagina of the sperm whale. *Cellular migration.* The
shifting meniscus of all touch. THERE IS NO SUCH THING AS
SKIN.

41. HOW WILL YOU BEGIN?

Take off your shoes. Take off your dress. Break the sage sticks into threads and drop them in the water. Sometimes I feel nothing. Sometimes I can't even make the word for nothing with my tongue and teeth and palate. *Put your fingers in your ears. Slide down into the green.* But I am not... I don't belong in this bloody bath. I just want to speak to him. *Him. Sit up. Shake your head until your hair is black. Rub your arms until they are red. Put on your dress.* It's raining. *I don't care. Put on your shoes. Do it.*

42. TELL ME WHAT YOU KNOW ABOUT DISMEMBERMENT.

When it rains, the grass is filled with blood.

I swore I'd never do anything so English as write about art. I said I'd write, instead, the book of blood. Chapter One: At the border, Hindu women are tied to Muslim eucalyptus trees. It is 1948, and so they are naked. Their wombs are hanging out of their stomachs. Chapter Two: there is no Chapter Two. I read the *Denver Post* — "According to our —" — and sip my tea; "— sources, the Serbs have made a practice of cutting out the wombs of women they rape, then hanging these wombs on poles."

I am writing because it is raining, and because there are many different kinds of rain. A Punjabi monsoon. The filthy spring-times of the European badlands. This rain, the mountain, the American, rain that's falling as I write, the rain that reminds me I am always facing East; the direction of water: its rapidly dissolving salt.

43. WHAT IS THE SHAPE OF YOUR BODY?

I rubbed an orange along the lines of my throat, to cool my blood. Am I alive? Yes. I am stretched out like the arms of a Hindu effigy, or an animal that lives in the sea. Sometimes, I'm scared I won't feel a damn thing. That is why I've stretched my body out. It's a net for a man. But a man is made of water. And I am pressed, face down, upon these boards. The muscles of my shoulders. My legs. *(But you cannot jump into the earth.)* Yes you can. Push harder.

44. WHO ARE YOU AND WHOM DO YOU LOVE?

Concise rooms: places to lay the head, submerged spaces. The water
is the light. That violet colour again, soaking through the gauze.
Windows. I hear his name in the Bulgarian chants I play when I'm
cleaning the room. Though it's been months. As if, all this time, I've
kept him inside me, like the semen that poured down my thighs
when I stood up. This room, its sloping ceiling. When I stand up, a
candle in one hand, book of matches in the other, I: can't. I don't
feel dizzy. I just sink. The floor is cold and hard: granite slab, sea-
bed, wooden boards shifting, miles from land; but something is
rising up my legs. A hum. I can't even begin. I can't even...

45. AND WHAT WOULD YOU SAY IF YOU COULD?

It's not enough. I'm running, I'm running across the street to the railroad tracks. *You are going to die when you are seventy-six years old.* Freight train coming. Standing on the white line, waiting for it to come. *Let it come.* It's coming. *When it comes, stand as close as you can. Step over the line. Stand with your legs wide apart, palms facing out in front of your chest. Eyes open.* Wooden boards. Blood in my hands. A face. A man, hunched above the shining metal, folded over. Paper. His eyes. Gone. Arizona. Oregon. Oil. Smoke. My ankles are shaking. I'm swaying. *Stop it. Don't look away. This is what you wanted. You wanted to begin. If you close your eyes, you will die.* But what about him? *That was him. Take the stone out of your shoe.* Keep walking.

46. DESCRIBE A MORNING YOU WOKE WITHOUT FEAR.

I've followed you as far as I can. To this ribbon of silver plastic, fluttering from a tree: innards of a tape you gave me: madrigals, etc. I threw it out the window last winter, at night, when the bone stars were rising in the trees.

47. WHERE DID YOU COME FROM /
HOW DID YOU ARRIVE?

My father arrives in Athens in 1961, hitch-hikes to Calais, takes the ferry to Dover, hitch-hikes to London, finds a cheap room in Golders Green. His first night in England, his landlady, a Russian Jew, asks him if he'd like some Welsh Rarebit. My father hears "Rabbit," and prepares himself for an exotic, hearty feast. When the cheese toast arrives, my father eats it in three mouthfuls, assuming that it is some sort of quaint appetiser. When the landlord pats his arm and says good night, *good night, deary,* my father is too embarrassed to bring up the subject of the main course.

48. WHAT ARE THE CONSEQUENCES OF SILENCE?

There are three kinds of hunger:

1.   I dreamed I gave birth to slab after slab of fresh meat, and that my mother held my feet down with her hands. When I woke up, I had an intense longing for the lentil soup my mother used to make, when I was sick, and home from school. Lots of lemon. Bay leaves. A spoonful of brown sugar. Something sweet and tangy at the same time.

2.   He is kissing your feet, your knees, your thighs. You reach down and pull him up to your mouth by his hair. This is a specific example of a hunger that is immigrant, in that you find yourself unable to ask for what you really want.

3.   The hunger that's made of eggshells: the most unstable version of the colour white. You are wearing chiffon. A sari made of magnolia petals. Your innards throb. For whatever reason, you will never see this person again. It is ten years from now. You wake up at four a.m., on the verge of panic.

49.   WHO ARE YOU AND WHOM DO YOU LOVE?

A back room at the A-1 Sweet Café, on the Southhall Broadway. My father and I are drinking *chai*, and eating *chaat*, while we wait for my mother to finish her grocery shopping at Dokal and Sons. We order extra onions and vinegar, and eat without speaking. I am sixteen years old. Nine or ten years later, when I am walking through a redwood grove on the coast of northern California, it is my father, eating steadily and ferociously, in the semi-darkness of a *dhaaba* in north-west London, who seems remote.

The distances between my body and the bodies of the ones I love: grow. They are limited by coasts. I have a few questions to ask, but I do not know how to break the growing silence. I breathe in the salty mist, walk back along the wild, shifting edge of everything.

50. WHAT ARE THE CONSEQUENCES OF SILENCE?

The afternoon I missed the bus and my friend's dad drove me home, I saw, approaching, that the glass of my front door was smashed. He asked me where I lived, and I lied, pointing out a neighbor's house, waving goodbye to him from its green and yellow wooden porch.

51.   HOW WILL YOU / HAVE YOU
   PREPARE(D) FOR YOUR DEATH?

Such open, such dark green hands. Walking along the edge of the mesa, she saw them: the yarrow pushing up, out of its own wrists, and then the sage. Green and yellow like that kept her safe: she could rub them between her fingers, bring her hands to her face, breathe in.

Later, in her room, she burned the sage, match by match, until the book was gone. That night she dreamed of her own hands, severed. In her dream, she fell asleep. When she woke, her hands had grown back. Instead of fingers, pale gold stems. Instead of nails, the tiny green alveoli of sage flowers.

When she woke, the sockets of her wrists felt watery: queasily, potentially, separable from the surrounding flesh.

52. WHAT DO YOU REMEMBER ABOUT THE EARTH?

My memories of violent acts are redundant. I am glad of predators. They remind me of the luxuriousness of heavy curtains. (Himachal brocades, cut-price velvet, hung up with drawing tacks.) Of waking in the dark and lighting votive candles.

Which is not to say I have not been a witness to the colours red, black, and white.

53. WHAT ARE THE CONSEQUENCES OF SILENCE?

Red Canna, I see you. Edge of. What I saw: a flower blossoming, in slow motion. *Not specific enough.* Okay. *No.* Cannot. Red Canna, I veer into you. I am not in one straight line. Red Canna, I see you. 1904. The University of Arizona Museum of Art. Opening in slow motion: are you okay? Are you okay? Can you hear me? (*I can't.*)

That's how it begins: impenetrable.

The book of two words I happen to see, out of the corner of my eye, on a wall. Such slowness.

These words took years to arrive.

54. HOW WILL YOU / HAVE YOU PREPARE(D) FOR YOUR DEATH?

Her first memory: the cool oak beneath her thighs. My mother was born in an India that no longer exists. The obsidian city of Lahore is now in Pakistan, and my mother's memory of a swing broad enough to bear the weight of forty cousins seems impossibly exaggerated. At the border, the women, tied to trees. Again and again, my grandmother pushed my mother's head beneath the sweet wet hay. But my mother saw this: a woman who had freed her arms. Although there were ropes around her lower body, the woman had not untied them. Instead she was praying, her fingers in a web across her face.

55. WHAT IS THE SHAPE OF YOUR BODY?

Federal Express, he sends me a photograph of a five-year-old girl.
She is wearing a Kashmiri chemise, and she has long black hair. He
has cut the face out. It is my face. The hole is the colour of my skin.

56. · WHAT IS THE SHAPE OF YOUR BODY?

The India House Restaurant. New York. My boss is behind the counter, counting out my tip money from the lunch shift. His tie, like my father's, is flung, as it always is, over his left shoulder, as if he walked here in high winds. It's late summer. His five-year-old daughter is fast asleep on the Persian rug behind the bar. She is wearing silk pantaloons, embroidered with gold butterflies, and a tank top.

Soft mouth open. Purple tongue. She's been eating licorice. She looks like a princess. Men, or women, will say it: you are my. But she isn't. She is the daughter of a restaurateur, just as I, in scarlet and silver taffeta, posing for a pale, bony-faced woman on a parapet at Windsor Castle, *Would you mind awfully?*, was once a daughter of a school-teacher who had recently arrived, *Your hair looks almost blue in this light, my dear,* in England. *Stay as still as you can.*

57. TELL ME WHAT YOU KNOW ABOUT DISMEMBERMENT.

We drank the colour blue from iridescent glasses. And thus, my life as I had known it, ended. Water. The high desert of Utah. Warped, diamanté drinking-ware from the 1970's. Whenever we stopped, he took off his clothes and asked me to photograph him, on scarlet-greenish precipices. The black hole of his nakedness, into which even distances shrank. Sank.

He writes, at an angle: *you exaggerate.*

5:30 a.m.:	having slept deeply, and stretched. Having drunk some blood. Having washed my face in smoke.
9:00 a.m.:	a manila envelope.
9:01 a.m.:	having opened it. The obliqueness of pre-memory. I know that the next minutes will turn into skin.
9:07 a.m.:	photocopied pages from my old notebooks. The most orange, untranslatable things I have ever said about my body. Marginal comments.
4:30 p.m.:	almost night. Already my thighs feel a little webby, and the skin beneath my eyes?: something inhuman. Plastic? Rubber. I pick at it.
1:01 a.m.:	I can't sleep. How will I live now, without eyelids?

59. HOW WILL YOU / HAVE YOU
   PREPARE(D) FOR YOUR DEATH?

SURGERY is often part of the treatment plan. Many patients have an operation called *œsophagectomy*. Generally, the surgeon removes a portion of the *œsophagus*, nearby *lymph nodes*, and other tissue in the area. Usually, it's possible to connect the *stomach* to the remaining part of the *œsophagus*. In a few cases, the surgeon forms a new passageway from the *throat* to the *stomach*, using tissue from another part of the digestive tract (such as the *colon*) to replace the *œsophagus*.

60. TELL ME WHAT YOU KNOW ABOUT DISMEMBERMENT.

"I miss your bones."

61. WHO ARE YOU AND WHOM DO YOU LOVE?

He's whistling, listening to carnival music, drumming his fingers on a coffee mug, and I feel trapped. How I met him, I was dancing. I was eating tomato soup. I was sobbing in a cathedral, with my eyes shut, when they sang. Bach sang. I was dancing, even though I didn't know how to.

A huge bruise on my left shoulder. The glamour of it. I tried to call him. PLEASE CALL YOUR AT&T OPERATOR. So I walked across the city, rang the bell. Here then, this. The edible paper of his body. I think of the ritual in a Hindu marriage, when the man and the woman stuff a silver-wrapped sweet-cake in each other's mouths. It makes you want to gag, but you have to. Gulp it down.

62. WHO ARE YOU AND WHOM DO YOU LOVE?

We drank tequila. We were *there*. Arrival: garlands of crumbling marigold petals, the slobbery upper arms. I don't know anything. He came. I rubbed it into him. It: everything spills. I realised then that I was greater than most people around me. (I could smell propane.) Because I knew when to shut my mouth. This all happened a long time ago. You are next to me, I said. *I want to tell you things.* I want to tell you things. I am not a business person. The tequila tasted of bad sea. Baggy-mouthed tetra. Tarred kelp. The good stuff. Not green, not black. *Gold*. Frozen. We ate our margaritas with a fork. He said, I've never seen anyone do that before. *Anyone. The good stuff. Crumbling.*

63. WHAT ARE THE CONSEQUENCES OF SILENCE?

I beg him to let me hold him. He doesn't want to hold me. He lets me hold him. I cry a little.

Today I came home with an egg-shell. Last week, I found a bull-snake's freshly shed skin next to the duck-pond. He says: *you keep coming home with exoskeletons.*

64.   WHAT IS THE SHAPE OF YOUR BODY?

I do not resist my death.

65. WHAT IS THE SHAPE OF YOUR BODY?

It was the summer I went to India by myself. We were high above the caves. We got off the bus and walked across the fields. I'll race you, he said. I took the path close to the edge. I turned the corner. A waterfall. A clear green pool. I took off my clothes and jumped in. I was seventeen years old. That morning, the blood of my first love-making was the shape of Australia. I'd known him for three days. I went to meet him in the third cave, my torso shining through my shirt. Look, he said. He was holding up a match. It was the wife of Buddha, naked to the waist, a flower between her fingers, staring back.

66. WHAT IS THE SHAPE OF YOUR BODY?

Punjab. Late spring. Sitting at the edge of my bed, I lean down to put my sandals on. Next to my sandals: a dark, hollow skin, as long and thick as a man's leg. The skin of a king cobra. When I touch it, the colour yellow explodes, at the base of my spine. Rises like shot, up, then out of me. Something that happened that morning: there is something in me, it must be met.

67. WHO IS RESPONSIBLE FOR
THE SUFFERING OF YOUR MOTHER?

(There is a new subject in the world.) New Orleans Museum of Art, 1995/ Monet's Garden, 1918. *These fragments will I shore/ against my.* But he, thigh-deep, wild white beard hanging down; in the border, paints: irises. The complicated dark between the stems. Saying: "But I need flowers, always, always." The human beings are in the shadows under a red willow, which is torqued and headless as the long body of an exploding man.

The subject is not the modern era, or the era we are living in now. The subject is not the metamorphosis of migrants, or the theory of limits, or the practice of seeing further into paintings. The subject is the human torso. Its dismemberment.

How much is enough? What is the bonded edge of…; my thumb-nails are throbbing. The theatre turns to paper: so many bright blinded faces. And when I come upon his corrections, in the margins of my old notebooks, something the size and density of a fresh fig turns, crunching, in the space above my stomach.

"The giving up of, again. Over and over, isn't it? Isn't it? Can't." And then, scrawled, in his delicate colonial script: *You are always pretending.*

Even this sentence is suspect: indefensible; potentially, already, rewritten. It's not even that. It's the bloodiness of remembering everything. I am bored of memory. I am bored of description. (My brain is too exposed. Old jelly. Inedible.)

69. WHAT ARE THE CONSEQUENCES OF SILENCE?/ AND WHAT WOULD YOU SAY IF YOU COULD?

The there–not-there image. A night that comes back to me only when I am awake. A temple in the desert in Rajhasthan. My uncle is the chief of police, and so we are hiding on the balcony. We are allowed to watch. When the doors are opened, the women burst in. They are naked, smeared with indigo and scarlet powders; leaping, chanting, eyes closed, faces contorted, streaming to the altar; collapsing into each other's arms. The priests begin to drum. Like the women, their faces are the faces I have only ever seen at night-time, when my lovers break open, and begin.

I want to begin. What is it like to *begin?*

70. HOW WILL YOU BEGIN?

I dream in HTML. The page shifts, doubles over, multiplies, vanishes. I think about writing in the ruled margins of my notebook, leaving the page blank as the centres of Hildegard's mandalas.

Nobody has died yet. I have not given birth to anyone. I understand that it will not always be possible to write this book. *My eyes are grainy. I haven't washed my hair in three days.*

The smell of sage and piñon in the smoke coming from the chimneys. I say: I want to live in an adobe house in New Mexico. I want to bake *naan*s in a clay oven, make love to a man with one eyebrow. January. The sound of rain on a metal roof. Moroccan cous-cous. He pushes my legs up for the first time.

I want to live according to this love. I wake in terror.

71. TELL ME WHAT YOU KNOW ABOUT DISMEMBERMENT.

If England is a test, then I have failed it. Train graffiti: "My dying bride." "Morbid angel." "As I die." "Bathory." The Satanists live in the suburbs. The remains of prayer. The last few chords: In the morning, a woman is begging, a baby strapped to her back. A piece of cardboard. Scored lines. "I am from Bosnia. Please help me. My husband is dead." Broke, I avoid her eyes. She moves on, into the salt light of the tunnel. Her body, her black size, beginning to fray.

(I am between whole numbers.)

72. WHAT ARE THE CONSEQUENCES OF SILENCE?

I am not writing about myself as a rational human being. I am writing about the substances of an animal and female life: magic, pain, the cracked nails of four feet, and the days like this one, when it is difficult to speak to a good-looking man. He returns with sesame seeds, unleavened bread, ginger and coriander powders, coffee, olives, chocolate, yoghurt, onions, cucumbers, potatoes, and a quart of milk. He thinks I am a woman because he bathes me, puts his hands on the sides of my face, tells me I am beautiful. Yes. Okay. But there is something hard between my lungs. It is the size of a blood-orange from northern California.

73. HOW WILL YOU BEGIN?

He writes / he said. The sloping off. An absence of epiphanies, despite the last, severed exchange. I asked a theorist what I should do. He said: numbness is a quality of transgression. I decided to eat an orange every day, for breakfast. In this way, I calculated that I would save $425 in groceries over the course of a year. In 1995, this was the price of a one-way ticket to Gatwick from JFK; non-refundable, coach-class, with the option of a vegan entree.

74. WHERE DID YOU COME FROM /
HOW DID YOU ARRIVE?

A real person: very rosy cheeks, a Yorkshire accent. Half Sikh, half English. When her parents moved to Paris, she had no reason to return to England. (It is the voice, not the skin, that says: I am without recourse to scones, or darjeeling tea, or raspberry jam, Robertson's, the kind with the little golliwog on the label. It is the voice, just the sound of it, words blurred, that says: I was not born — dead, double-dead, very dead, dead, dead, dead, dead, — here. (*But I am happy in Colorado.* The body descends. Without any fuss.))

75. WHAT IS THE SHAPE OF YOUR BODY?

William Takamasu-Thomson, a Japanese-American war-baby from Kansas, playing conga drums and snake-rattle, in a Chicano jazz-band, in the rented club-house of the Fraternal Order of Eagles, Fort Collins, Colorado.

Perhaps I have not been making the body of a woman, but the body of

Ergo: The man's body constitutes the negative space that is ostensibly generated by the excision of — what? — *the woman's* — I beg your pardon? — *throat box.*

76. AND WHAT WOULD YOU SAY IF YOU COULD?

A photograph of André Malraux in a camel-hair dufflecoat, smoking a bony Gauloise, frowning. I thought I'd put it up in honour of the summer night a man pulled off the Taft Hill Road into a cow-field, turned up the radio, handed me a Nat Sherman, and knew the names of the stars. (The sweet, paper-wet systole. Our sudden, filmy clumsiness with the matches. Is there a verb for: going further with?)

But it's my *father*: the ratty, toggled dufflecoat he wore twenty winters in a row. The Silk Cuts he stopped smoking, abruptly, in 1983. This winter, back from the Big Sur, I call home. His voice sounds different. Scratchier. He says it's snowing.

My night. His morning. He's drinking tea with crushed cardamom pods in it, and honey, to soothe his throat-chords. It's snowing in London for the first time in years. His chemo starts on Tuesday. (Verb No. 1: to colonise. An obliterating whiteness.)

77. HOW WILL YOU LIVE NOW?

Unpacking, I sometimes stare at the words that fall from books. The scraps. *Will I plead with you to come live with me in forests of azure. Will I beg you to leave me.* There are no question marks. First night alone, I fall asleep in a bed of papers: uncreased, separated, placed in piles. When my mother first left Pakistan, she couldn't take her diaries. And so she burned them. Keeping the ash in little lacquered boxes tied with string. In India, she cut the string and placed the shiny black boxes on a shelf in her new room, that she shared with her mother, who was waiting for her husband to arrive, who didn't arrive until the next winter, the long bone of his right arm shattered, unable to speak.

78. WHAT ARE THE CONSEQUENCES OF SILENCE?

I'm writing this on my side, at noon, in the basement, on the carpet, in front of the space heater. Page 79 or 80 or 81. I have not said one thing about what actually happened between us. Sometimes I think that all the books about what actually happened have already been written. That the only book left is the book of a refugee who has never left the country of her birth: written: on the torn-out pages of old comic books — *Batman, Bunty, Tales From The Crypt* — with invisible ink, and held, with shrimp tongs, above the burner.

(Recipe for Invisible Ink: A solution in which the insoluble residue sinks to the bottom of the beaker. For example, sugar-water. In which separation occurs as descent, not evaporation. The sugar is delicious. You can make yourself a nice cup of tea with what's left over. Step two: Or mix with egg whites. Stiffen. Add hot water, and bingo. Chopsticks make convenient, disposable writing utensils for shorter messages.)

79. WHAT IS THE SHAPE OF YOUR BODY?

I took notes. But once, after the first few months, he stole my note-book, tore out the pages with all the sexual sentences, photocopied them. *His yellow teeth. His Nick Cave albums. His love of eggplant parmesan.* And so there are gaps. A surprise ending: and then I see him again, and my whole body is full of spicy eggs. *The tangles of my menstrual hair. The swell of my lower body.*

I can smell myself. "I knew this woman," he said, "Her vagina smelled of flowers. Have you ever considered using a douche?" I met him in the spring. Walking home along the canal bank, I'd snap off tiger buds. *Lily heads, and eat them.* They tasted good, but I got the shits.

80. WHAT IS THE SHAPE OF YOUR BODY?

Fall Landscape No. 3: leaving Wyoming and returning to Colorado: the bluffs of blue and orange hills curl over, then stop, mid-break. The moon is rising. Eyeball moon: the black curve as visible as the shining one. Orange rock with lime-green algae and silvery water-stains. Stretch marks. Stainless steel clips from an abandoned climb. Climbed way up. Leaned forward in the wind, free-falling on the spot.

Revision No. 2: it is time to describe the body. I am a woman in the same way that my mother was a woman: a little paranoid. At the border, they will ask you for your notebooks. (The desecration of notebooks.) A red vinyl suitcase filled with brightly-coloured dresses, and hand-stitched dolls. (The scraps.) It is 1947. It is 1948. My mother is just a little girl. (And the flash of white bobby-socks? Clock faces.)

81. WHAT IS THE SHAPE OF YOUR BODY?

There are phones ringing, beyond Beethoven. It is eleven in the morning, and already the day has backed up farther and farther inside me. Today I cannot shake the lump of coal out of my body. The man goes to the supermarket to buy some milk. The music turns left. The words stop. Only the horns remain. When the key turns in the lock, only my eyes move. Eyeballs.

82. TELL ME WHAT YOU KNOW ABOUT DISMEMBERMENT.

Double Vision: I am as old as my mother was when she arrived in England to live with her new husband. There's a photo of her taken that first winter: she's standing between the two apple trees in the garden, shivering in the silver paper of her sari. I am inside her. My father is grinning. My mother looks away at the last moment: her face blurs.

Anti-vertigo tablets. Half a bottle left. Every time I lift my head, I feel nauseous. One long spiky and flaking branch has snapped a bit, jutting out towards the window of my bedroom. I stare at it for hours. It moves from side to side, very slowly, like an old boat. It leans into the living tree that is thick with its swollen, rattling pods. I am going to have to heal myself.

83. HOW WILL YOU / HAVE YOU
     PREPARE(D) FOR YOUR DEATH?

Of your mouth. No eyes. Of your left breast in his mouth. The fat
kiss. Of his twitchy face, when he knows he must gulp it down, bear
down upon the sweetness: otherwise. It will be too much.

The snow comes in waves. I can't even move my head. My eyes are open. The catalpa pods are singing. The sound of tongues slapping the roofs of fifty or sixty mouths.

Moves through the glass. Into the bones of my skull.

My left arm is tingling. When I lift my head off the pillow, the window-pane rises and falls: Turns into a viscous — a body — luminous — of light. Running.

85. WHO IS RESPONSIBLE FOR THE SUFFERING OF YOUR MOTHER?

1. An initiatory interstices

She died in the time of jade: during the few days in early April, when trading was at its most intense. In the interior minutes of a shop-keeper's afternoon, when the stone was pushed across the glass, again and again, then wrapped in blue tissue paper and tied with red silk — it was Easter; ribbons.

(and pressed into hands that resembled all other hands, the briefly impervious varnishes of their nails, and the broken Girdles-of-Venus beneath the third and fourth fingers, on the palm-side — indicating:

an electrical, a pollen-sharp — a sensitivity: to the edible heart of things:)

she died.

86.   AND WHAT WOULD YOU SAY IF YOU COULD?

The night before I married the bicycle mechanic — a man who, when I met him, offered me his skull, to cup its birth-bumps in my palms; our first touch — I dreamed of an owl. An owl-man, swaying from foot to foot, in the dark beneath the pines, behind the Morgan-Manning house. His eyes, bright yellow. No irises. No eyelids.

Beneath, behind. There are names for it, then. Names that tell us how to get there — entering at dusk, our shoulders hunched over, ducking; eyes lowered like brides, not all brides; uncertain women dressed in red silk, the colour of the morning sun; forced into it: the double kingdom.

And so I left my bed, dressed swiftly in black, and walked to the little grove between State Street and Main. I knew there would be owls: all Summer and then the Fall, I'd stood at the doorway of my house, in the evening, to listen. Sometimes, my

It is not enough to describe this longing. René Char is dead, but his poems have been made into Mexican love-songs. I think people are starting to realise that it is a little unbearable to travel such distances, so swiftly: on Saturday, in South Kensington, I met a man from America. He was carrying a brown leather satchel with many pieces of loose, creamy-grained paper in it. Love letters. A black looped script. Addressed to a woman in Madrid. He talked slowly about this woman, breaking off to look at the moon. "My girlfriend lives…in Madrid." "She…edits advertisements…for a horticultural magazine." "Her eyes?" "Her eyes…" "Her eyes are…" Green.

With bits of brown in them. Longing is vague. "This longing..."
Is vagueness that prevents you from entering the body of your
lover / being entered. Better to stay put. Linger and sputter over
the Giacometti torso of your lover. Your strung-out lover who is
waiting for you to harden / to evaporate. (Sometimes, the bicycle
mechanic would light candles on his front doorstep, before leaving
the house. Even he, the oily one, the one who had stacks of *Pent-
house* and *Playboy* in a box under his bed, longed for the actual
angel, the dubious one who would nevertheless: take him, into her
jaggedy mouth)

body: he tells me that I have her mouth. Somebody's blurry
mouth. And I run my tongue from right to left and back again,
along the irregular ridge of my lower teeth. Peach string. The taste
of bone. To be real. Listening.

(The night I went to the owls, my husband was drinking Labbatt's
in the C and S Saloon, playing eight-ball with the Mexican migrant
workers, on their last night before they headed south. Standing in
the doorway, the last stubs of votive candles melting into the cold
step, I stretched back until my heart bone snapped: walked out into
the gold and black night. The barest structure of relief. Smell of
damp leaf mulch in the crisp air.

(Hü.)

Standing beneath the pines all night: "this longing is enough."

I forgot this. I forgot my life.

I knew a man who made tea from animal juices. He had wonderfully strong yellow teeth. (His semen came out in clumps. It made me gag. When the tea was ready, he'd squeeze the bag with his fingers and lay it on the table cloth.)

The morning, the last three or four hours, before I met him, I was walking through the park with a five-year-old girl. To the greenhouse, where the scarlet fish glowed beneath the five or six or seven surfaces of the water, and the bananas were dark green. Half-notes: She tells me that she loves hot buttered toast with strawberry jam. When we hear the sound of bells, she says, "That's where God lives." This is the only text of this hour. He has torn out all the night-time sentences. *There were red fish. Sight bent like tin.*

I met him in the diner on the corner of Prince and Elizabeth, at 2:30 p.m., on December 1, 1993. I mean April. It was the morning. I ordered tomato soup, and a cup of earl grey tea. No milk. Milk. Milk? Honey.

(The future: his books. Hundreds of them. Spanish, Marathi, Dutch. I can't read them. Impenetrable lushness of a library in other languages. How will it be possible, I used to think, to give myself over to such translation? What is necessary now? What is happening?)

Coming out of the park onto the street, I notice a carcass. Raccoon, split open. Look!, I say to Shanta, pointing behind us, and up, to the sun. But she smells the blood, and looks.

88. WHO IS RESPONSIBLE FOR
   THE SUFFERING OF YOUR MOTHER?

For two rupees, I buy a boat of palm-leaves. I want to make the shape of my mind and body. The crumpled dark of my lower intestine. The films of Fellini, dubbed or undubbed. I want to write about the woman who takes a walk one Spring evening, in the once-a-year rain, in the high desert, in her antique wedding dress; Spanish chiffon, twenty pounds, sterling. Bad mango: I wanted to make a document of this time in history. Its paranoid states.

89. WHO ARE YOU AND WHOM DO YOU LOVE?

OUT: "Who am I? Where is my love? Where is my food?"

IN: "It is colder in my home than it is outside. Everyone I love is away. There is a tiger sewn inside your belly. This is good. Your lover is somewhere that Whitman hasn't covered. You will find him in a place that he left out. *Who am I?* There is nothing that doesn't bring you to this edge. *Where is my love?* Your love is underneath the sun. *Where is my food?* It is in your tongue."

90. WHAT ARE THE CONSEQUENCES OF SILENCE?

His hair was often the colour of the underside of peacock-feathers: a rather dull brown. That Fall, walking across the city to meet him, my eyes grew orange flecks. I have never felt more brave, more invisible.

Each meeting is the same meeting. Say what has to be said, in order to stay alive.

"What do you write about me in your journal? Go on, then. Tell me something."

"No."

"Why?"

"Because I'm a spy."

"So?"

"So I have to keep my mouth shut."

And yet, I find myself, twitchy, beginning each sentence at the top of each page.

The bed I'm making, the bed I've made. Underneath the bed, I find the old beach-towel we used to wipe ourselves with, after love-making. I think about it, but I don't do it.

91. HOW WILL YOU BEGIN?

I'll begin with his feet. The way he walked all night, in the rain, looking, he said, for a cave. Finally, in a rock-face, he saw a fissure. Closer, he saw it was just a pine, snapped at the top and bent over into its own shadow.

The whiskey's in my chest like a boat. The under-darkness, the emptinesses, of the hold. *Stand up.* He pulls down my trousers with one hard tug. First night in the new room, I dream of swans. Swans, these bare walls, and how eggs streamed from womb to womb. The damp bed-sheet. Womb: anything that gives itself up. Swans: it darkens and darkens. Gods flicker.

92. WHAT ARE THE CONSEQUENCES OF SILENCE?

Finally, I'm alone. No dress. No shoes. No black bra. I am not a box.
We talked all night, stroking each other's torsos. (Legless, beheaded.)
The same old chat.

Excised: *His blue coming. My knee-sockets crack. And kneeling, I close
my eyes.* He has a mosquito bite on his right thigh. How can I speak
about this? *With my hands.* But the only sign I know is the one for
song:

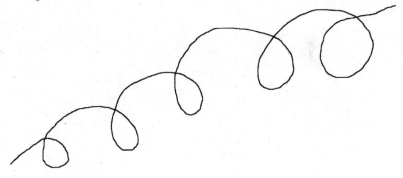

It resembles barbed wire.

93. HOW WILL YOU LIVE NOW?

A physiology of abrupt severance: I miss his bones. I miss him in my hair and in my nails. (Red from pressing down, hard, with black pens. Yellow-white with a citrus texture: my fingertips. And loose, my hair, its length, is intolerable. I stick pins in it.) A keratin loneliness, then: when a pulse is felt, even in the dead parts of oneself.

94. HOW WILL YOU / HAVE YOU PREPARE(D) FOR YOUR DEATH?

The unexpected lake: blue-white ice-slabs almost to the edge. Moving isthmus of bright blue water. Little rivers within that still. The evening sun behind us. A canal, shade-filled, to our left, below us. To our right, the shore of the lake: spongy crust, and a bank of orange-red willow wands. We walk through the dry gold grasses, up to our thighs in the world. Black yucca seeds. I press one into the skull of a craw-daddy: the exoskeleton of its face and foreclaws, poking up, out of the mud.

95. HOW WILL YOU BEGIN?

When I was fourteen years old, my father and I climbed The Old Man of Coniston, a small mountain in the Lake District. At the top, a tourist from Peking takes our photograph, in which we grin, our arms around each other's shoulders. Then the man takes a photograph with his own camera. Our bright faces, then, muttering and chafing in the dark of a lacquered box, somewhere in China. The dark of my father's forehead growing darker.

It is another ten or eleven years before we sit together in the kitchen, drinking red Bulgarian wine, the milk from the yoghurt boiling on the stove, my father getting up to stir it, every ten minutes or so, with a wooden spoon. We drink the whole bottle of wine together, for the first time in our lives. It is enough, at last.

96. WHAT IS THE SHAPE OF YOUR BODY?

But it's not enough.

97. WHO IS RESPONSIBLE FOR THE SUFFERING OF YOUR MOTHER?

When my mother's uncle was dying, I went to his house to say goodbye. I was twenty years old. When he saw my face, he started crying. My mother said it was because I looked so much like his sister, Shanta, who had died when she was nineteen. She bled to death when she climbed the mountain behind her house. My mother said she should never have gone for a walk when she had her menses. I knew immediately, I don't know how, that she had died, hæmorrhaging, during a miscarriage. That she had climbed the mountain on purpose. But nobody would ever say that.

(Shame may be fatal)

98. WHAT DO YOU REMEMBER ABOUT THE EARTH?

Steam rising from the cracks in the asphalt. I do not think I will die today.